FRANCIS AND eddie

the true story of america's underdogs

WRITTEN BY BRAD HERZOG   ILLUSTRATED BY ZACHARY PULLEN

Special thanks to author Mark Frost for bringing this story to life
so brilliantly in *The Greatest Game Ever Played* (Hyperion, 2002).

Text copyright © 2013 Brad Herzog
Illustrations copyright © 2013 Zachary Pullen
Designed by Lindsey Grant
Edited by Aimee Jackson

Printed and bound in the
United States of America
First Edition
LCCN 2013931128
ISBN 978-0-9849919-2-1

Why Not Books
831 Spruce Avenue, Pacific Grove, CA 93950
www.whynotbooks.com

JE

One sunny September morning in the quiet village of Newton Lower Falls, Eddie Lowery crept along the platform at the trolley station. He glanced left and right until he spotted a truant officer patrolling the area. Eddie crouched low, which wasn't difficult. At the age of ten and only four feet tall, it came naturally. He had been warned not to skip school that day—by the officer and, even worse, by his mother. But they didn't understand. He had to get there.

Sneaking from spot to spot, he finally slipped into the last trolley car. It was headed eight miles east toward the town of Brookline, Massachusetts, and one of the world's great golf tournaments—the 1913 United States Open.

As the trolley rumbled along, Eddie remembered how he and his brother had first practiced golf by using umbrellas as clubs and crab apples as balls. They tried to imitate the swing of Francis Ouimet, a young man who had recently won the state amateur championship.

Twenty-year-old Francis Ouimet lived with his family in a little house across the street from The Country Club in Brookline. His hard-working father worked as a gardener for the wealthy club members. Arthur Ouimet dreamed of such riches for his son Francis, though he was certain the golf course was not the place to find them. But Francis loved the game. He taught himself how to play by practicing in his backyard cow pasture.

Although he owned only one golf club as a child, Francis found lots of golf balls. Once he even discovered a treasure—a ball emblazoned with the words "VARDON FLYER." Harry Vardon was a pro golfer from England who had already won the British Open five times. He was the best player on the planet, and now Francis was about to compete in a tournament with the great man himself!

Nobody believed an unknown amateur like Francis had a chance to win, not even his regular caddie, who had decided to work for another golfer instead. Eddie Lowery's older brother, Jack, had carried Francis's golf bag during a practice round. But now, only ten minutes before Francis was scheduled to attempt to qualify for the tournament, Jack was nowhere to be found. As Francis stood on the practice green, little Eddie came running up to him.

"Where's Jack?" Francis asked.

Trying to catch his breath, Eddie said, "He had...to go...to school."

"So why aren't you in school?" Francis said.

Eddie's eyes widened. "This is the U.S. Open," he said.

Francis started to walk toward the first tee, figuring he would carry his own clubs. Eddie followed him.

"Mr. Ouimet," he said. "I could caddie for you."

Francis smiled and shook his head. "My bag's as big as you are."

"I can do it, Mr. Ouimet. Really I can!" Eddie insisted. "I can help you out there. I know your game. I can carry this bag."

Francis had once been a caddie himself, and he knew that experience was more helpful than enthusiasm. But he saw a look in the boy's eyes. Eddie was determined. "All right then, let's go," said the young man, handing Eddie his bag. "Just please call me Francis."

Francis got off to a terrible start. His first shot nearly went out of bounds. After two shots, he was still 220 yards away from the hole. He looked nervous, so his little caddie gave him some big advice. "Keep your head down, and I'll watch the ball," Eddie said. "I've never lost a ball yet."

Francis's next shot landed on the green only twenty-five feet from the hole. "Eddie," he said, handing the club to his caddie, "I think you and I are going to be good friends."

Francis then played magnificently. He finished with the second best score of the day, behind only Harry Vardon. Many newspapers printed headlines about the local "kid" who qualified for the U.S. Open by playing so well. Francis's mother and sister saved the articles and started a scrapbook, but his father ignored them. *Golf,* Arthur O thought, *is not how my son will achieve a better lif*

The first two rounds of the tournament were played on Thursday. Once again, Eddie slipped into a trolley car and rode to Brookline. He arrived to find nine thousand spectators. Most of them were there to watch the famous Harry Vardon. But as Francis began to play well, his crowd grew.

"This kid's for real," Eddie heard someone say after Francis made a ten-foot putt.

"You bet he is," said Eddie.

At the end of the day, Vardon was tied for the lead. Close behind him was another Englishman and former British Open champion, Ted Ray. He was a mountain of a man who hit the ball so far that it seemed to disappear into the sky. But Francis was only four strokes behind.

On Friday morning, Francis woke to rain. Still, he grabbed his golf clubs. He was excited to play the final two rounds of the tournament. Francis walked out his front door to find his smiling caddie holding a black umbrella. "Eddie, it's a fine day for golf," said Francis. "Let's have some fun."

Francis's mother hugged him, and his sister and brother told him they would be following him on the course. But his father simply muttered, "Playing in the rain today."

While most of the golfers played poorly in the wet weather, it felt familiar to Francis. He used to sneak onto the golf course and practice in the rain when he was younger. Francis birdied the first three holes, improving his score by one stroke each time. The crowd cheered louder and louder. As Eddie walked quickly along the fairways, trying to keep up with Francis, fans reached out to pat each of them on the back. It was as if the spectators wanted to touch a miracle in progress. After three rounds, three men were tied for the lead—Harry Vardon, Ted Ray, and young Francis Ouimet.

Thousands of spectators whooped and hollered, tossing their hats and umbrellas into the air. It was certainly the loudest celebration ever in Brookline and probably ever in American golf.

The news quickly spread worldwide. The amateur golfer from across the street had matched the best of the best. Francis finished his round tied with Vardon and Ray, and tomorrow he would face off against them in a playoff. When he stepped inside his house, Francis saw his father, still in his mud-caked gardener's clothes. Arthur Ouimet had heard the chorus of cheers all day. A man of few words, he simply told his son, "You did well today."

Eddie and Francis made quite a pair on Saturday morning before the playoff began. They wore matching boots and ties as they strolled toward the golf course beneath a light drizzle of rain.

Each day throughout the tournament, Eddie had predicted that Francis was going to shoot a score of 72. "I saw it," he explained, "like in a dream." It hadn't happened yet, but now he said it again. "Today's the day," Eddie announced. "It's your last chance."

As Francis stood on the practice green, his friend Frank Hoyt approached him. "You ought to have somebody carrying your bag who really knows the game and the course," Hoyt said.

"But Eddie's done a wonderful job for me," Francis replied.

"He's a fine little kid. But this is for the U.S. Open," Hoyt said. "I should carry for you today."

Hoyt offered Eddie five dollars to give up the bag, a large amount of money in those days. But Eddie refused it. "I wouldn't do it for a hundred," the boy told Francis, wiping away a tear. "I'm the caddie."

Francis smiled and turned to Hoyt. "I truly do appreciate your offer, Frank, but I've already got the man I want on my bag."

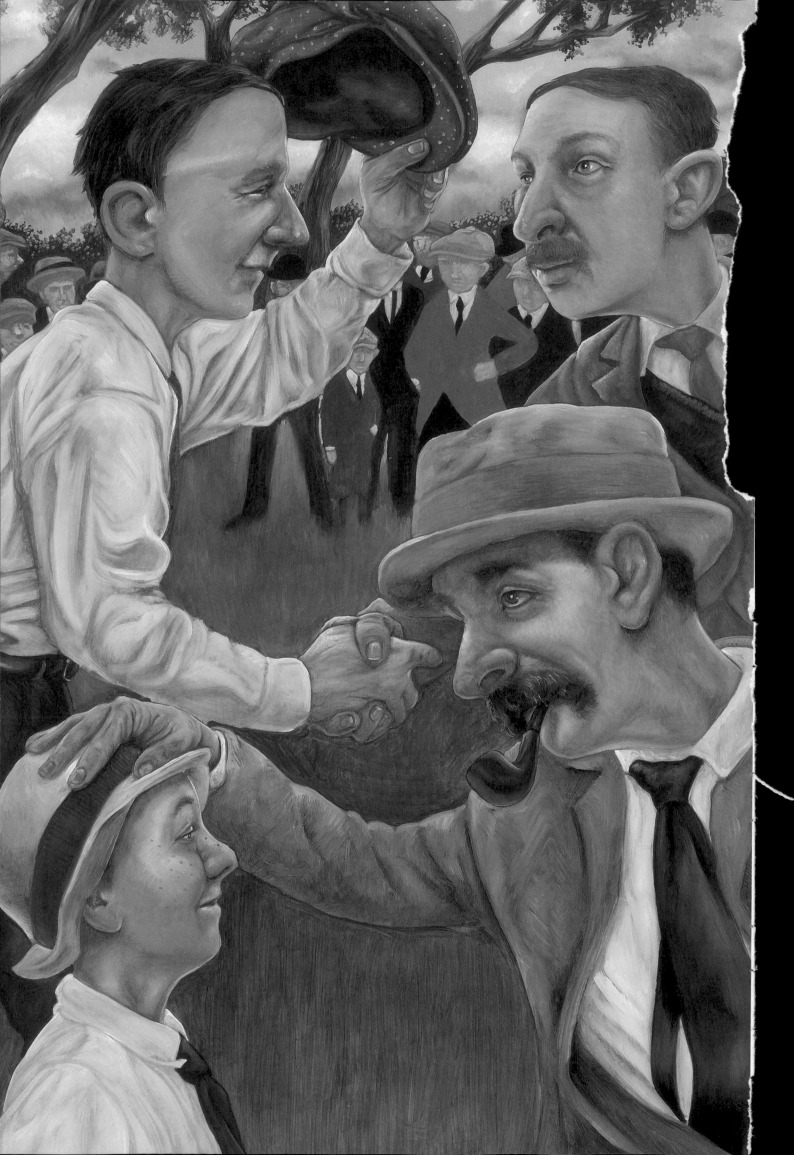

Surrounded by a massive crowd at the first tee, Francis shook hands with his famous opponents. Ted Ray looked down at the ten-year-old caddie. "What's your name, little man?"

"Eddie Lowery."

"Eddie, you're not much bigger than a peanut."

"That's okay," Eddie replied. Then he made the crowd laugh by adding, "You're big enough for both of us."

After the first nine holes, the three men were tied. Each had shot even par. Francis actually began to believe that he might have a chance.

"I can play with these guys, Eddie," he whispered.

"Who said you couldn't?" the boy replied.

But it turned out that Francis could play better than the other guys. He was in the lead by two strokes when he stood again on that same seventeenth green. Francis glanced at his little house across the street. It was less than a hundred yards to his front door, but it seemed like he had come such a long way.

Francis studied the task in front of him. This time, it was an eighteen-foot putt. If he made it, there was almost no way he could lose.

"Take all the time you need," Eddie told him.

Francis took a deep breath and then barely nudged the ball. It seemed to roll forever, but when it finally stopped, it was in the bottom of the cup. For the next few minutes, Eddie wondered if they could hear the cheers all the way across the Atlantic Ocean.

Francis tapped in his final putt on the eighteenth hole, beating the great Harry Vardon by five strokes and powerful Ted Ray by six. Hundreds of fans rushed toward him. They lifted Francis onto their shoulders and reached out to touch him. People even held up money, a reward for the thrill he had given them. But Francis shook his head. He wasn't a professional, so he couldn't accept a dime.

But Eddie could.

"Pass the hat for Eddie!" Francis shouted. Suddenly, his little caddie was being lifted, too, and grinning from ear to ear.

Francis watched as a man pushed through the crowd and placed the very first dollar into the hat. The man had tears in his eyes as he looked up at the young champion. It was Arthur Ouimet, bursting with pride.

Later, Francis sat on a bench in the clubhouse locker room. His champion's trophy was beside him. As usual, so was Eddie, who stared in awe at the gleaming silver cup.

"How much do you have there?" Francis asked.

Eddie held a roll of folded bills. "Almost a hundred dollars," he said. "That's more money than I've ever seen in my whole life!"

"I want you to have this, too," said Francis. He handed him one of the two golf balls he had used that day. "I think I was able to do what I did here because you believed I could."

Eddie took the ball and examined it carefully. Then he looked up at the man who would become his lifelong friend and grinned. "We shot 72."

"Yes," Francis smiled, "we did."

AFTERWORD

Francis Ouimet (pronounced "we-met") and his U.S. Open triumph elevated golf into a major sport in America. Francis never became a professional golfer, but he won the National Amateur Championship the very next year in 1914. Seventeen years later, he won it again. Francis was one of the original inductees into the World Golf Hall of Fame, but he considered his greatest achievement to be the Francis Ouimet Scholarship Fund. Since 1949, it has provided more than $25 million to help thousands of caddies and students pay for college.

As for his famous caddie, one newspaper reporter described Eddie Lowery as "the most envied and happiest boy in Newton." He became a very good golfer himself. In 1927 he won the Massachusetts Amateur Championship, and Francis watched him do it. Although he began his career as a sportswriter, Eddie eventually became a very wealthy businessman and a longtime supporter of amateur golf.

Each year, the Ouimet Scholarship Fund honors a person chosen as the top caddie of the year. The winner receives the Eddie Lowery Award.

If you or your parents would like to learn more about Francis and Eddie and the incredible 1913 U.S. Open, please read Mark Frost's comprehensive book about the event — *The Greatest Game Ever Played* (Hyperion, 2002).